STACEY
ABRAMS

STACEY
ABRAMS

CHAMPION OF DEMOCRACY

DR. ARTIKA R. TYNER

LERNER PUBLICATIONS ◆ MINNEAPOLIS

Lerner Publications Company
An imprint of Lerner Publishing Group, Inc.
241 First Avenue North
Minneapolis, MN USA 55401

For reading levels and more information, look up this title at www.lernerbooks.com.

Image credits: REUTERS/Phil McCarten/Alamy Stock Photo, p. 2; AP Photo/Brynn Anderson, p. 6; Alyssa Pointer/Atlanta Journal-Constitution via AP, pp. 8, 11; AP Photo/John Bazemore, pp. 9, 32; Brian Cahn/ZUMA Wire/TNS/Alamy Stock Photo, p. 10; Bob Andres/Atlanta Journal-Constitution via AP, pp. 13, 19, 33; Jonathan Goldberg/Alamy Stock Photo, p. 14; AP Photo, pp. 15, 16; Mike Levitt/Invision for Girl Scouts via AP, p. 18; Andre Jenny/Alamy Stock Photo, p. 21; Atlanta Journal-Constitution via AP, pp. 23, 25; Nick Arroyo/Atlanta Journal-Constitution via AP, p. 24; David L. Harris/Library of Congress (LC-DIG-ppmsca-70889), p. 27; f11photo/Shutterstock.com, p. 28; Sandra Baker/Alamy Stock Photo, p. 29; AP Photo/David Goldman, p. 31; Bill Clark/CQ Roll Call via AP, p. 34; Michele and Tom Grimm/Alamy Stock Photo, p. 35; REUTERS/Brendan McDermid/Alamy Stock Photo, p. 36; 7partparadigm/United States Department of the Interior/Wikimedia Commons, p. 37; AP Photo/Ben Gray, p. 38; Senate Television via AP, p. 39; 52nd NAACP Image Awards/BET/Getty Images, p. 40.

Cover: Jamie Lamor Thompson/Shutterstock.com.

Main body text set in Rotis Serif Std 55 Regular. Typeface provided by Adobe Systems.

Library of Congress Cataloging-in-Publication Data

Names: Tyner, Artika R., author.
Title: Stacey Abrams: champion of democracy / Dr. Artika R. Tyner.
Description: Minneapolis: Lerner Publications [2022] | Series: Gateway biographies | Includes bibliographical references and index. | Audience: Ages 9–14 | Audience: Grades 4–6 | Summary: "Stacey Abrams is a lawyer, entrepreneur, and voting rights activist. After working in government, she founded Fair Fight Action to improve voting access. Learn about Abrams's early life and what she plans to do next"—Provided by publisher.
Identifiers: LCCN 2021035870 (print) | LCCN 2021035871 (ebook) | ISBN 9781728441849 (library binding) | ISBN 9781728448787 (paperback) | ISBN 9781728444734 (ebook)
Subjects: LCSH: Abrams, Stacey—Juvenile literature. | Black women politicians—Georgia—Biography—Juvenile literature. | Politicians—Georgia—Biography—Juvenile literature. | Legislators—Georgia—Biography—Juvenile literature. | Suffrage—United States—History—21st century. | Black legislators—Georgia—Biography—Juvenile literature.
Classification: LCC F291.3.A27 T96 2022 (print) | LCC F291.3.A27 (ebook) | DDC 975.8/044092 [B]—dc23

LC record available at https://lccn.loc.gov/2021035870
LC ebook record available at https://lccn.loc.gov/2021035871

Manufactured in the United States of America
1-49939-49782-9/15/2021

TABLE OF CONTENTS

Stacey Abrams addresses supporters of Democratic presidential candidate Joe Biden in November 2020.

n November 2018, many eyes were on Georgia's gubernatorial race. The election saw Democrat Stacey Abrams face off against Republican Brian Kemp. As the final votes were counted, Kemp led Abrams by a little less than fifty thousand votes. Kemp beat Abrams to become the next governor of Georgia. It was one of the closest statewide races in recent US history.

The nation awaited a final concession speech from Abrams. She was known as a young, ambitious, and visionary leader. Many dreamed she would transform Georgia. During her campaign for governor, Abrams created a plan to increase funding for children's education. She wanted to expand access to health care for everyone. Her plans encouraged small business owners to grow, supported criminal justice reform, and aimed to improve access to mental health services.

After the results of Georgia's 2018 race for governor came in, Abrams voiced concerns that the race had not been conducted fairly.

Abrams sparked interest in voting and civic engagement across the nation. She reminded everyday people that their voices mattered. They could help to shape laws and policies on issues from immigration to criminal justice. They could serve their communities to transform local schools and economies. She challenged citizens to take action to build stronger communities and brighter futures.

On November 16, 2018, Abrams stood at a podium at her campaign's headquarters in Atlanta, Georgia. Her supporters gathered to listen, and people from across the nation and the world watched as the speech was broadcast. Abrams looked into the camera and began to speak, starting with the history of voting and democracy.

Abrams also referred to concerns that the race for governor was not conducted fairly. Kemp ran for office while he was Georgia's secretary of state. One of his duties was to oversee elections. This meant Kemp both oversaw and ran in the same election. During the race, his office removed over a half million voters from Georgia's registry. His office also blocked fifty-three thousand new voters from voting. These actions created challenges for voters hoping to register and cast their ballots.

Brian Kemp in November 2018

Many Georgia voters faced long lines on election day.

Voters in Georgia faced more difficulties on election day. Some polling places were closed, while others were short of paper ballots. Polling stations were overcrowded, and lines to vote were long. People waited in lines for hours, some for as many as eight. Others had their ballots thrown out if their signature did not match the one on their original voting registration card. Many were confused about how to vote by mail through an absentee ballot and how to vote in person. People were also given mixed messages. Abrams herself was initially told that she could not vote in person since she had requested an absentee ballot. But she had never applied to vote absentee. Voting machines malfunctioned. The list of issues continued to grow.

Abrams said that Georgia had failed its citizens. "More than 200 years into Georgia's democratic experiment, the state failed its voters," she said. "Let's be clear—this is not a speech of concession, because concession means to acknowledge an action is right, true or proper." She encouraged everyone to take a stand for democracy by ensuring fairness in elections and voting rights for all. She said the future of Georgia was in their hands.

Many believe the issues with the election caused Abrams to lose the election. Some believed they were examples of voter suppression, or strategies to intentionally

Abrams with her nephew, Cameron McLean, after casting her vote in 2018

make voting difficult. But Abrams still made history by running for governor of Georgia. She was the first Black woman to receive a nomination for governor by a major US political party.

Abrams had hoped this would be only one of a series of trailblazing moments. She would have been not only Georgia's first female Black governor but the first in the United States. And she would have been the first Democrat to win a statewide race in Georgia since 2000. But Abrams is still making history as she registers a record number of voters, supports the creation of better job opportunities, and works to ensure everyone is counted in the US Census.

Family Roots, Family Values

Stacey Abrams was born on December 9, 1973, in Madison, Wisconsin, to Robert and Carolyn Abrams. Stacey was their second child out of six. When Stacey was young, her family moved to the South. Stacey spent her early years in Gulfport, Mississippi. Her family lived in Gulfport until she reached middle school.

Stacey grew up with deep connections to her family. Her parents worked hard to build a strong and successful life for their children. Her father was a shipyard worker, and her mother was a head librarian. Though their family had little money, Stacey's parents taught all their children about the importance of high expectations. Stacey

Abrams and her parents as she began her campaign for governor in March 2018

and her siblings were encouraged to dream big, pursue their education, and serve their community. Stacey and her siblings learned from their mother the importance of reading and writing. The family enjoyed learning, watching PBS specials, and reading books together. As a childhood pastime, Stacey liked to read the encyclopedia. It was her opportunity to learn about a wide range of topics and unleash her imagination. She could travel the world and explore history. Also at an early age, Stacey discovered her gift for writing. She started writing and never stopped, going on to write several novels as an adult.

Modeling the way for their children, Stacey's parents were serious about education for themselves too. The family moved to Georgia so her parents could continue their schooling. Both attended Emory University and earned graduate degrees in divinity. Their strong belief in serving others led them to become United Methodist ministers.

Stacey's family experienced hard times. Yet they persevered. When they were unable to pay their bills, the water was cut off. Stacey's mother referred to this jokingly as "urban camping." No matter the challenges they faced, Stacey's parents reminded her that having nothing is no excuse for doing nothing.

Service was a big part of their lives. The family served in the community together. They volunteered at soup kitchens and helped the homeless. They volunteered together at prison outreach programs and at polling places during elections. Stacey and her siblings were taught three

The Abrams family prepared meals for those in need in kitchens like this one.

key values: go to school, go to church, and take care of one another. They also were assigned an important job. If they saw someone in need, Stacey and her siblings had to help that person.

The family also served in the community by promoting civic engagement and equal rights. Stacey's grandmother taught her the importance of voting. She reminded Stacey of Black people's long struggle for voting rights. In 1870 the Fifteenth Amendment

Black voters casting ballots in Mississippi in 1967

to the US Constitution granted Black men the right to vote. However, states then created laws to enforce racial segregation, or the separation of Black and white people. These Jim Crow laws included requiring people to take literacy tests and pay poll taxes to vote. One law called the grandfather clause said that people could vote only if their grandfather could vote before the Civil War. These laws intentionally created barriers to voting for Black men.

Black women fought in the movement for women's voting rights. They hoped their efforts would lead to not only gender equality but also to racial justice. The Nineteenth Amendment granted voting rights to women in 1920. But for Black women, the amendment's passage did not mean they could actually exercise these rights. In the face of restrictive voting laws, both Black men and women saw the harsh truth that the promise of equal rights did not include them.

Black people fought for their voting rights for generations. During the Civil Rights Movement, they marched and protested for justice. On March 7, 1965—later known as Bloody Sunday—voting rights activists organized a march from Selma, Alabama, to Montgomery, Alabama, to protest the unfair treatment of Black voters in the state. Future congressional representative John Lewis led more than six hundred people to march across the Edmund Pettus Bridge in Selma. They were brutally beaten by state troopers.

Finally, in 1965, the Voting Rights Act was

Martin Luther King Jr. (*right*) leads a march for voting rights in 1965 alongside fellow civil rights leader Ralph Abernathy (*left*).

signed into law. Stacey's grandmother voted for the first time three years later. She put on her best clothes to go to the polls. At first, she was afraid to cast her vote. She remembered how Black people had been beaten, sprayed with fire hoses, bitten by dogs, and even killed for trying to vote. But she overcame the fear of retribution by thinking about the future. She understood her vote was her power to make a difference, and she believed that she owed it to her children and the following generations to use that power. After that first vote in 1968, Stacey's grandmother never missed an election.

The Voting Rights Act of 1965

The Voting Rights Act of 1965 was signed into law by President Lyndon B. Johnson. It outlawed discriminatory practices that restricted access to voting. But in 2013, one piece of the act was struck down by the Supreme Court. This piece required states to earn outside approval to change certain voting practices. With this oversight, states had more difficulty creating laws intended to exclude certain voters. Without it, many believed creating discriminatory laws would become easier.

Unstoppable

Stacey learned early never to give up. In the mid-1980s she was selected by her Girl Scout troop leaders to represent Mississippi at a Girl Scouts national conference. Some community members were unhappy that a Black girl was selected. They tried to make sure that she didn't make it to the conference by changing her flight reservation and leaving her behind. But Stacey was unstoppable. She flew by herself to the national conference in Arizona.

Stacey's parents also helped to prepare her for the difficult road ahead. They did not want her to let adversity convince her to abandon her dreams. "Let other people

Girl Scouts aims to teach girls civic responsibility as well as leadership and practical skills.

Abrams's parents, the Reverend Robert Abrams (*front left*) and the Reverend Carolyn Abrams (*right*), continue to be big influences in her life.

tell you no," her father told her. "Never tell yourself no. If there's something you want, fight for it." This wisdom guided her studies and continues to guide her career. Stacey knew her destiny was greater than anyone could imagine. She learned to tell herself, *Yes, you can!*

The Girl Scouts experience and other experiences taught her to keep pressing forward during difficult challenges. During her campaign for governor, she reflected on the lessons she had learned: "There are going to be a lot of people who try to stop you from getting on that plane. There are a lot of people organizing themselves to make sure I land at the wrong destination. There are folks who don't think it's time for a Black woman to be governor of any state, let alone a state in the Deep South. But there's no wrong time for a Black woman to be in charge." During her race for governor, Abrams drew upon the strength she showed as a young girl. She kept her final destination in clear focus. She was determined to fight for justice and build a stronger Georgia.

Top of the Class

Stacey was an excellent student. When she was a junior in high school, she earned a high score on the PSAT. This precollege exam prepares students for the SAT. It also identifies top-performing students from across the nation. Based on her score, Stacey was selected for the Telluride Association Summer Program. This is a prestigious summer program for high-achieving youth. She attended the program with some of the brightest students in the nation.

The experience initially felt overwhelming. She realized the other students had had different privileges and access to opportunities than she had. It was difficult for her to compete, and she called her parents to ask if she could return home. But her parents made her complete the program. Stacey decided not to let anyone intimidate her and make her give up. She learned as much as she could from her peers.

After she finished the program, her ambition and confidence grew. She was determined to make her dreams come true. She later referenced the Bible to write,

"Proverbs tells us that iron sharpens iron. So too does ambition sharpen ambition. Dreams hone other dreams." The summer program prepared her for the future as she dared to dream bigger.

At eighteen Abrams graduated from Avondale High School in DeKalb County, Georgia, with honors. She was the highest-achieving student at her school and was named the valedictorian. In Georgia the governor sends a special invitation to high school valedictorians for a meeting at the governor's mansion. Abrams traveled to the other side of town with her parents to attend the special celebration. Her family could not afford a car, so they took a bus. A guard at the gate of the governor's mansion watched them as the bus pulled away. As Abrams and her family approached, he told them that they did not belong there.

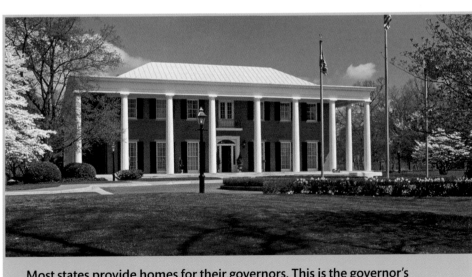

Most states provide homes for their governors. This is the governor's mansion in Atlanta, Georgia.

Abrams's father confirmed that she was being recognized as one of the state's high school valedictorians. Her mother opened her purse and retrieved the invitation to try to show the guard. He ignored them and repeated that they did not belong there. Eventually, he looked at the list, saw Abrams's name, and allowed them to join the event. But the experience set the stage for Abrams's future career. She was determined to create opportunities where there was a true sense of community. She would help to create places where everyone knew that they belonged, that their voices mattered, and that they had the power to shape their destinies.

Spelman Bound

Abrams had an important decision to make: where she would attend college. She had spent most of her life in the South, but she wanted to go to school in the North. Her mother's dream had been to attend Spelman, a historically Black women's college in Atlanta, Georgia. But she could not afford to attend. Abrams's mother convinced her to apply to the prestigious college and make her unfulfilled dream a reality.

After Abrams was admitted to Spelman, she took a day to visit the school. Spelman is the oldest historically Black college for women. Abrams saw that the school was committed to inspiring Black women to change the world. She envisioned herself becoming part of a rich legacy of high-achieving Black women leaders. Though she had wanted to go to school in the North, she decided to attend Spelman.

Spelman College

Founded in 1881, Spelman College is one of a group of historically Black colleges and universities (HBCUs). These schools were created to educate Black students when many were barred from higher education. Spelman was founded specifically to educate and inspire Black women. Important women such as author Alice Walker, children's advocate Marian Wright Edelman, activist Bernice King, and business leader Rosalind Brewer graduated from Spelman.

Abrams at Spelman in 1992

While at Spelman, Abrams excelled academically. She emerged as a natural leader and used her voice to make a difference. She was named a Harry S. Truman Scholar in recognition of her academic success and commitment to public service. As a sophomore, she decided to become a student leader. She organized her campaign and was elected vice president of student government. During her junior year, she applied for the prestigious Rhodes scholarship. The scholarship allows students around the world to earn fully funded graduate degrees at the University of Oxford in England. Abrams was the first Black woman from Mississippi to be chosen as a candidate. Many told her that the distinction meant she was likely to succeed at the national level. But she was not chosen for the scholarship. She later reflected upon this experience, stating, "Losing prepares you for success." Abrams learned that she had to be willing to take a risk and strive to reach her goals. Losing the scholarship helped her to overcome the fear of failure.

Abrams was determined to stand up for what was right no matter what. Sometimes this meant taking risks and going up against powerful people. During Abrams's junior year of college, the first Black mayor of Atlanta, Maynard Jackson Jr., visited Spelman to hold a town hall. Abrams publicly challenged Jackson over his record on social justice issues. The move could have backfired, but instead, Jackson was impressed. He later created an Office of Youth Services

Maynard Jackson Jr. (*center*)

and hired Abrams to be a member of his team. She was the only undergraduate student on the staff, demonstrating her leadership skills and setting her apart from her peers.

In 1993 Abrams was selected as a youth speaker at the thirtieth anniversary of the March on Washington. She drew upon the leadership legacies of President Abraham Lincoln and Martin Luther King Jr. She challenged her listeners to focus on how young people could help to build a road to better jobs, justice, and peace. She dispelled the myth that young people had to wait to lead, insisting that age does not determine what someone can achieve. Abrams created a vision of shared partnerships between young people and adults in creating change. Future generations could not afford to wait for the promise of equal rights and justice to be realized. The work must be done today.

During her college years, Abrams launched her first voter registration campaign by recruiting her friends to vote. She convinced them of the importance of voting, emphasizing it as a key way to use your voice in a democratic society. Abrams also attended city council meetings and zoning meetings to study government and policy-making in action. She worked to have the Confederate emblem removed from the Georgia state flag. For many, the emblem is a reminder of racial terrorism and violence against Black people dating back to the Civil War and earlier. Her and others' advocacy led to the flag being changed. Each of these experiences provided Abrams with the tools to inspire, motivate, and organize others. She used these tools throughout her career.

The March on Washington

The March on Washington was in August 1963. Organized by civil rights leader A. Philip Randolph, the march's purpose was to demand good jobs and freedom for Black people. More than 250,000 people gathered in front of the Lincoln Memorial in Washington, DC. King delivered his famous "I Have a Dream" speech. Other prominent leaders in the Civil Rights Movement also spoke, including Bayard Rustin, National Association for the Advancement of Colored People president Roy Wilkins, John Lewis of the Student Non-Violent Coordinating Committee, organizer Daisy Bates, and actors Ossie Davis and Ruby Dee. Iconic singers such as Marian Anderson and Mahalia Jackson performed.

Abrams graduated with honors with a bachelor's degree in interdisciplinary studies (political science, economics, and sociology) and a minor in theater. Spelman provided her with a strong foundation to build her future. She decided to continue her studies and pursue a graduate degree.

The Young Lawyer

In line with her commitment to public service, Abrams earned a master's degree in public affairs from the Lyndon B. Johnson School of Public Affairs at the

The University of Texas's Lyndon B. Johnson School of Public Affairs is named after the thirty-sixth US president.

Yale University in New Haven, Connecticut, is one of the most prestigious schools in the US.

University of Texas at Austin. Her education there gave her the tools to transform government policies. She decided to attend Yale Law School to learn more about law and how to use it to create change. After graduating in 1999, she returned to Atlanta and became a tax attorney at the law firm Sutherland, Asbill & Brennan. From 1999 to 2003, she practiced tax law with a focus on tax-exempt organizations and public finance. At twenty-nine, Abrams was appointed the deputy city attorney for the City of Atlanta. She oversaw legal and policy analysis for the city's transportation and key economic development initiatives. She managed a team of more than twenty attorneys and paralegals.

Lawyers Leading Change

When Abrams decided to attend law school, she knew that lawyers have shaped the course of history. They can serve as leaders who seek justice and protect the rights of the people. Charles Hamilton Houston (1895–1950) is one lawyer who made a difference. He laid the groundwork for the case of *Brown v. Board of Education* (1954) that ended racial segregation in schools. Barbara Jordan (1936–1996) was a lawyer, professor, and public servant. She was the first Black woman elected to the Texas State Senate and the first southern Black woman elected to the US House of Representatives. She advocated for better wages and labor laws to protect workers.

Working for the People

Abrams's commitment to public service and the betterment of society compelled her to run for office. She was elected as a state representative in Georgia. She served eleven years in the Georgia House of Representatives, seven as the Democratic leader. In 2010 Abrams became the House minority leader for the Georgia General Assembly, making history again as the first woman from either party to do so. She was also the first Black woman to lead in the House.

Abrams remembered what she was taught as a little girl about service and helping others. She worked across the aisle with Republicans to serve the needs of the people of Georgia. She helped to prevent a large tax increase that would have created financial hardship for many Georgians. She helped to improve public transportation. She helped to save important scholarships for students in need. She worked with then Republican governor Nathan Deal to promote criminal justice reform.

Abrams is committed to helping people understand the power they have through voting. Before she ran for governor, she created the New Georgia Project, a voter registration organization. Between 2014 and 2016, her team helped more than two hundred thousand people of color register to vote.

Abrams speaks in Georgia's House of Representatives in 2016.

She continued to connect with people and learn their stories. She encouraged them to shape their destinies by becoming civically engaged. Abrams sought to create an atmosphere where all Georgians knew they belonged. Drawing upon her experience more than twenty years earlier of not being welcomed at the governor's mansion, she decided to open the gates of opportunity to everyone. No matter one's race, gender, class, or educational attainment, everyone would be included in building a more just and inclusive Georgia.

Abrams ran for governor of Georgia in 2018, losing by a narrow margin. The election was one of the closest statewide races in recent history. After the election, Abrams sat shiva for ten days. Shiva is a period of grief

Abrams inspired many in her fight to become Georgia's governor.

Abrams works at a Fair Fight phone bank in Atlanta in 2019.

and mourning in Judaism. She then began to strategize about her next move. She was determined not to allow what many believed were voter suppression tactics to influence an election again. She founded Fair Fight Action, a national voting rights organization, in Georgia.

Fair Fight focuses on democracy-building through the power of voting rights. The organization fights to end voter suppression and ensure accountability in elections. It uses three strategies. The first is litigation. Fair Fight files lawsuits when it believes that voters have been treated unfairly or that officials have behaved unlawfully. The second is legislation. The organization works to create policies that ensure everyone has equal access to the ballot box. The third is advocacy. Fair Fight works with communities to support civic engagement and voter participation. Through its efforts, the organization hopes to provide people with the tools to understand their voting rights and their important role in US democracy.

Another issue Abrams focuses on is the US Census. The Census is an effort to count every person living in the US. The count happens every ten years. The Census shapes the future of a community. It decides which communities receive federal funding, how much money they receive, and how much political representation an area gets. Abrams knew it was critically important to make sure that everyone was counted.

Abrams continued to collaborate with Georgia's House of Representatives as part of her work with Fair Fight.

The US Census

Being counted in the US Census helps your community to get the resources it needs. Census numbers are used by federal and state governments to decide how to spend money on things like schools, health care, and fire departments. Money also goes to Medicaid (medical aid for those who can't afford it), food assistance, housing assistance, and school lunch programs. Census numbers also determine fair political representation. For example, the Census determines how many congressional representatives each state has in the US House of Representatives.

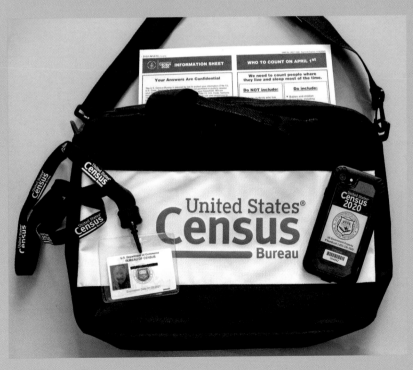

In 2020 Census workers often went door to door to collect information about American households.

The Census count is conducted through forms where people fill in information about themselves. But some may not want to give the government personal information. And some groups of people may be difficult to locate or contact. Due to concerns about communities of color, rural communities, and other historically oppressed groups being undercounted, Abrams founded Fair Count. The organization worked to ensure that these communities were counted in the 2020 Census.

In 2019 Abrams launched the Southern Economic Advancement Project to promote economic growth and prosperity in the southern US. The project focuses on improving the lives of marginalized communities in twelve southern states. Its work involves creating good jobs, supporting families, protecting the rights of workers, and offering access to better education.

A Call to Leadership

Abrams is a strong strategist and problem solver. She outlines her goals and ambitions and then creates an action plan to implement them. She asks herself three key questions: What do I want? Why do I want it? And how do I get it? She wants to end voter suppression. Daily, she takes actions to reach this goal. Her journey was documented in the film *All In: The Fight for Democracy* (2020). The film explores her 2018 campaign for governor and the work of her organization, Fair Fight. The film also puts a spotlight on voting in the US. It illustrates how tactics such as poll closures, voter intimidation, registration purges, and strict voter ID requirements suppress votes. Another tactic the film covers is gerrymandering, or the drawing of legislative districts to favor one political party over another.

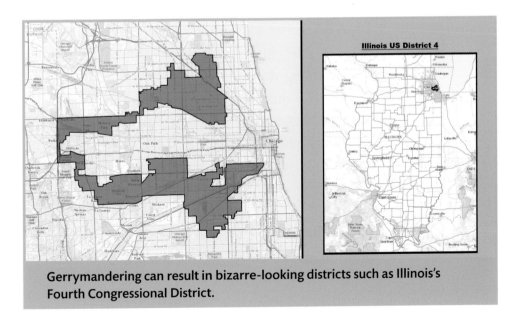

Gerrymandering can result in bizarre-looking districts such as Illinois's Fourth Congressional District.

Abrams and Senator Amy Klobuchar of Minnesota led a roundtable about voting rights in July 2021.

Finally, the film explains the need for improving the voting process and ensuring voting access for everyone.

Leaders help to build a vision for the future. They work with others who share the same values and ambitions to achieve their goals. Abrams's leadership focuses on her commitment to a strong democracy and equal voting rights. Her vision is to mobilize the collective power of ordinary people. In this vision, everyday people shape their futures through the power of the vote. "In this country, democracy is how we speak to those in power and how we determine who holds power. And that's my mission," she said.

Abrams has combined her vision with action. During her postelection speech in 2018, she said, "Put America on notice: change is not coming to Georgia. It has arrived." Through her hard work and organizing efforts, she increased voter participation and support of the Democratic Party in Georgia. Many southern states are represented mostly by Republicans. But in 2020, Abrams worked to register record numbers of voters in Georgia and across the nation. She used a boots-on-the-ground approach to organize volunteers, who in turn inspired people to get registered to vote. In Georgia more than eight hundred thousand new voters registered. Perhaps as a result, Democrats greatly increased their representation in Georgia's government. Two Georgia Democrats, the Reverend Raphael Warnock and Jon Ossoff, were elected US senators. And for the first time in more than twenty

New registered voters helped elect two Georgia Democrats to the US Senate. On January 20, 2021, Raphael Warnock (*left*) and Jon Ossoff (*second from right*) were sworn in.

Stacey Abrams in 2021

years, a Democratic presidential candidate won Georgia's electoral votes. Many credit Abrams's leadership for these historic achievements.

Many wonder what's next for Abrams. She is a dynamic, zealous advocate for justice and a globally recognized leader. In 2021 she was nominated for the Nobel Peace Prize for promoting nonviolent change through voting and civic engagement. She is the award-winning author of eight romantic suspense novels, with total sales of more than one hundred thousand copies. Her most recent book, *While Justice Sleeps*, is a legal thriller. Abrams is also an entrepreneur who creates businesses to address social challenges. She is the cofounder of Now, a financial services company that focuses on helping small businesses grow. In every part of her career, she uses her creativity and critical-thinking skills to address complex challenges.

The Nobel Peace Prize

From 1901 to 2020, 603 Nobel Prizes have been awarded to exceptional people around the world. Nobel Prizes are awarded in six categories: physics, chemistry, medicine, literature, economic sciences, and peace. The Nobel Peace Prize has been awarded to leaders such as US president Barack Obama and Liberian president Ellen Johnson Sirleaf, the first female elected head of state in Africa. It is intended to recognize efforts to increase peace by reducing armed conflict, encouraging cooperation between nations, promoting human rights, and more.

Each day, Abrams helps to write a new chapter in the history of the United States. Her dream is to lead the US as president. In an interview, she said that she hopes to become president by 2040. Meanwhile, she will keep making history and fighting for liberty and justice for all.

IMPORTANT DATES

1973   Stacey Abrams is born on December 9 in Madison, Wisconsin.

1991   She graduates from high school as her class's valedictorian.

1992   She joins a student protest at the Georgia State Capitol to speak against the use of the Confederate emblem on the state flag.

1995   She graduates with honors from Spelman College.

1998   She earns a master's degree from the Lyndon B. Johnson School of Public Affairs at the University of Texas at Austin.

1999   She graduates from Yale Law School and becomes a tax attorney.

2002   She is appointed deputy city attorney of Atlanta.

2007   She begins to serve in the Georgia House of Representatives.

2013 She creates the New Georgia Project, a voter registration organization. The nonprofit helps more than two hundred thousand community members register to vote between 2014 and 2016.

2017 She makes history when she launches her campaign for governor of Georgia.

2018 She founds Fair Fight Action, a national voting rights organization, in Georgia.

2019 She launches the Southern Economic Advancement Project to promote economic growth and prosperity in the southern US.

2020 She founds Fair Count to ensure that communities of color, rural populations, and other marginalized groups are accurately counted in the 2020 Census.

2021 She is nominated for the Nobel Peace Prize for her work in promoting voting and civic engagement.

SOURCE NOTES

11 Gregory Krieg, "Stacey Abrams Says 'Democracy Failed' Georgia as She Ends Bid for Governor," CNN, November 17, 2018, https://www.cnn.com/2018/11/16/politics/stacey-abrams -concession/index.html.

14 Ariel Goronja, "Stacey Abrams' Parents: 5 Fast Facts You Need to Know," Heavy.com, February 5, 2019, https://heavy.com /news/2019/02/stacey-abrams-parents-mom-dad-family/.

18–19 Michelle Darrisaw and Samantha Vincenty, "14 Things to Know about Stacey Abrams," Oprahdaily.com, November 6, 2020, https://www.oprahdaily.com/life/a24749080/stacey-abrams -georgia-governor-race-condede/.

19–20 Amelia Poor, "One-on-One with Stacey Abrams," Scholastics. com, May 17, 2019, https://kpcnotebook.scholastic.com/post /one-one-stacey-abrams.

21 Stacey Abrams, *Lead from the Outside: How to Build your Future and Make Real Change* (New York: Picador, 2018), 8.

25 "Stacey Abrams Tells Oprah Winfrey 'Losing Prepares You for Success': Watch News Videos Online," Global News, November 1, 2018, https://globalnews.ca/video/4619942/stacey-abrams-tells -oprah-winfrey-losing-prepares-you-for-success.

38 Adelle M. Banks, "Stacey Abrams' Zeal for Voting Began with Preacher Parents," Associated Press, October 17, 2020, https:// apnews.com/article/race-and-ethnicity-religion-stacey-abrams -georgia-voting-rights-9bef13d7118801d8adc9055a33ac1a76.

38 "Full Speech: Stacey Abrams Ends Candidacy for Georgia Governor," YouTube video, 12:01, posted by NBC News, November 16, 2018, https://www.youtube.com/watch?v =G1YXTP7u8Ds.

SELECTED BIBLIOGRAPHY

Associated Press. "What Are Voting-Rights Advocate Stacey Abrams's Plans for 2022?" MarketWatch. Updated April 23, 2021. https://www.marketwatch.com/story/what-are-voting-rights-advocate-and-nobel-peace-prize-nominee-stacey-abramss-plans-for-2022-01619044105.

Aviles, Gwen. "Stacey Abrams Has Been Fighting Voter Suppression for Years." *Harper's Bazaar*, November 6, 2020. https://www.harpersbazaar.com/culture/politics/a34599550/stacey-abrams-facts/.

Garcia-Navarro, Lulu. "A Constitutional Quirk Inspired Stacey Abrams' New Thriller, 'While Justice Sleeps.'" NPR, May 9, 2021. https://www.npr.org/2021/05/09/994605989/a-constitutional-quirk-inspired-stacey-abrams-new-thriller-while-justice-sleeps.

History.com editors. "Jim Crow Laws." History.com, March 26, 2021. https://www.history.com/topics/early-20th-century-us/jim-crow-laws.

Krieg, Gregory. "Stacey Abrams Says 'Democracy Failed' Georgia as She Ends Bid for Governor." CNN, November 17, 2018. https://www.cnn.com/2018/11/16/politics/stacey-abrams-concession/index.html.

"Stacey Abrams for Governor." Join Stacey Abrams. Accessed July 18, 2021. https://staceyabrams.com/.

"Stacey Abrams Spoke in 1993 at the Anniversary of the March on Washington." NowThis News. Accessed July 18, 2021. https://nowthisnews.com/videos/politics/stacey-abrams-spoke-at-the-anniversary-of-the-march-on-washington.

"Stacey Abrams: 'The Anguish Is Real' | Where Do We Go from Here?" YouTube video, 2:29. Posted by OWN, June 9, 2020. https://www.youtube.com/watch?v=m_QTi6ir_Hw.

Taylor, Jessica. "Stacey Abrams Says She Was Almost Blocked from Voting in Georgia Election." NPR, November 20, 2018. https://www.npr.org/2018/11/20/669280353/stacey-abrams-says-she-was-almost-blocked-from-voting-in-georgia-election.

Webster, Emma Sarran. "Stacey Abrams, Candidate to Become Georgia's Governor, Talks Fear, Failure, and Power." *Teen Vogue*, May 2, 2018. https://www.teenvogue.com/story/stacey-abrams-candidate-to-become-georgias-governor-talks-fear-failure-and-power.

LEARN MORE

Bartoletti, Susan Campbell. *How Women Won the Vote: Alice Paul, Lucy Burns, and Their Big Idea.* New York: HarperCollins, 2020.

Chambers, Veronica. *Finish the Fight! The Brave and Revolutionary Women Who Fought for the Right to Vote.* New York: Versify, 2020.

Kiddle: Stacey Abrams Facts for Kids
https://kids.kiddle.co/Stacey_Abrams

Library of Congress: The Right to Vote
https://www.loc.gov/classroom-materials/elections/right-to-vote/

Stacey Abrams
https://kids.britannica.com/kids/article/Stacey-Abrams/633174

Tyner, Artika R. *Black Voter Suppression.* Minneapolis: Lerner Publications, 2021.

INDEX